ALL THE KING'S THINGS

THE ULTIMATE ELVIS MEMORABILIA BOOK

This 1993 edition published by
Bluewood Books
A Division of The Siyeh Group, Inc.
111 Pine Street, Suite 1410
San Francisco, CA 94111

Printed and bound in Hong Kong

ISBN 0-912517-04-2

9 8 7 6 5 4 3 2 1

How did it happen? From what ethereal spring did this, the most incredible phenomenon of the Global Pop Age, originate? It started in another time, another place. It was a time much like our own, but at the same time, very different. Imagine you're driving through the South in the 1950s. Your way is marked by the old white US Highway shields, not the red, white and blue of the Interstate signs. The place names crop up on little white signs, not those huge green things. Memphis. Jackson. Tupelo. Shreveport.

It gets awfully hot in the car, so you swing into one of those little roadside cafés for a glass of iced tea. My, but it's cool inside. They've got one of those little glass cases with all the pies displayed, and goodness, doesn't the banana coconut chiffon look good!

As you leave, and push through the screen door, a big Cadillac with a bunch of boys in it pulls up. You chat a bit and they tell you they're headed to Shreveport to sing on the radio—on the Louisiana (pronounced lōō′ zē-ana) Hayride. You wish them well and promise to tune in.

We all tuned in. That's how it all happened.

Photography: Ming Louie
Art direction and staging: Richard Michaels and Bill Yenne
Text and design: Bill Yenne
Staging crew: Brenda Arlene Butler, Lauren Michaels, Tina Louie,
Robin Rosaaen and Lisa Marie Yenne
Motorcycle: Tom Debolski

CONTENTS

WELCOME

When **Elvis Aron Presley** sang *Welcome To My World* there was always an immediate bond between him and the audience. It was as though he were inviting *us* to become part of *his* world, and to join him in a special, indescribable way. He touched our lives and we can never forget him.

In this book, we welcome you to the world of Elvis memorabilia thoughtfully collected over the past three decades by **Robin Rosaaen**. While nothing can ever take the place of the kind of closeness that we experienced being in the same room with Elvis, spending time with Robin's collection evokes many memories and special feelings. Indeed, this was our motivation for producing this book. We wanted to share Robin's special collection with the rest of the world and have a little fun at the same time.

Robin Rosaaen has been an Elvis fan since she first saw him on television when she was a little girl, and she has been a collector of memorabilia since that day so long ago when she saved her nickels and dimes and bought her first Elvis 45 rpm record. It was *Jailhouse Rock*. From that humble start she has amassed stacks of wax, miles of tape and thousands of Elvis-related items of every imaginable description.

She saw him in concert 72 times and came to be known to Elvis and his entourage. He started calling her **Rockin' Robin** and he would always recognize her when he saw her in the audience. Without question, her most treasured possession is the few strands of **his hair** that got caught in her ring as he leaned down from the stage to give her a kiss and a scarf. She is in touch with a worldwide network of Elvis fans that range from members of the King's original entourage to Raisa Gorbachev.

From her first records, and her first Elvis bubble gum cards, to locks of his hair, to a rose from his casket, Robin's collection has grown into one of the largest private collections of Elvis memorabilia in the world. Indeed, according to California's *Peninsula Times Tribune*, it is the largest collection anywhere outside Memphis, Tennessee. She has appeared in dozens of newspaper articles, as well as on many radio and television programs, including *The Oprah Winfrey Show* and *The Geraldo Show*. Each time, however, there was neither time nor space to begin to show even a tiny fraction of the more than 40,000 items that Robin has amassed.

We wanted to give fans everywhere access to a larger slice of Robin's collection in a way that allows both the time and space to enjoy it.

We've designed this presentation in a way that we hope you'll find enjoyable and entertaining. Rather than display this memorabilia in a

stark, museum setting, we've chosen to make each display *interactive*. Your voyage of discovery will reveal many exciting artifacts from the life of the King that are hidden in the rich tapestry of memorabilia. You will experience the fun of finding new things every time you look at the pictures.

Each display is based on a theme or a particular facet of Elvis' life. You've already seen Robin's **garage** pictured on page one. On the wall there are **license plates** from all three of the states where Elvis lived for any length of time after he and his folks moved from Tupelo, Mississippi in 1948 when he was 13. Can you find them? One of these is Robin's old plate, and there's a clue as to *which* one is hers later in the book.

As you turn these pages, you'll find a cornucopia of Elvis memorablilia. There are scenes devoted to **his films**, **his music**, and his fascination with **Hawaii**. We'll even take you into Robin's **kitchen**, where fried peanut butter and banana sandwiches are *always* on the menu.

When you've had a chance to explore each of these scenes, you might like to go back and try to find the RCA mascot **Nipper** pictured a total of eight times, with **hound dogs** and **teddy bears** *each* pictured or mentioned 22 times. There is also *one* item which appears in **every** two-page photograph in this book. Can you find it?

We hope that you'll enjoy this tour through this truly unique collection and have fun exploring each of these images again and again!

THE YOUNG ELVIS

Elvis Aron Presley was born at 12:20 p.m. on January 8, 1935 in a small wood frame house on Old Saltillo ("Saltville") Road in Tupelo, Mississippi. This scene is a tribute to his early years—from that afternoon in 1935 to his breakthrough as the greatest singing sensation in history. The map here shows the route that he and his parents, Gladys Love and Vernon Elvis Presley, took when they moved to Memphis, Tennessee in September 1948.

The **house in Tupelo** where Elvis was born is pictured five times and his parents, **Gladys** and **Vernon**, and his manager, **Colonel Tom Parker**, are each pictured once. His high school graduation picture is in the middle. The picture of **Elvis with a pistol** is from the years from 1949 to 1953, when he and his family lived in Lauderdale Courts at 185 Winchester Street in Memphis. Do you see his **birth date** mentioned twice and the **year he graduated** from high school mentioned three times? His high school girlfriend, **Barbara Hearn**, is pictured twice. She's all alone, but Elvis is pictured here with his arms around **eleven other gals** and **one guy**. Can you spot them?

It was just a few months after he graduated from Humes High School that he went into the Memphis Recording Service to cut a record for his mama's birthday. He went back a few weeks later, in January 1954, to record two more songs. This time, Sam Phillips, who owned both Memphis Recording Service and **Sun Records**, heard him and signed him to a recording contract. Elvis' popularity took off like a rocket. There are no rockets here, but there are four **Sun records**. The **Sun logo** appears six times. Can you find all these?

One of Elvis' logos was the **hound dog**. Can you see a hound dog mentioned or pictured on these pages six times?

The **cap** and the **bubble gum cards** all date from 1956, when his career was just starting to take off. As you can see, the cards used to go for a nickel a pack. Can you imagine what they'd be worth now? Can you find one of the cards that refers to **Elvis by a different name**? It is the character he played in his first movie, *Love Me Tender* (1956). Deborah Paget played his wife, Cathy Reno.

A ZILLION GOLDEN RECORDS

No rock star ever had a recording career like **Elvis Aron Presley**. In over 20 years of performing, he had more than 137 gold and platinum records, but there are only ten **gold records** in *this* display, which is our special tribute to his musical career. He started out on the **Sun Records** label in 1954, but he switched to **RCA** in 1955.

Nipper is RCA's mascot, and the little dog appears twice in this scene. The centerpiece of our display is from **Elvis' August 1956 Tour**, when he was at the absolute peak of his career. The circular sign is from the **1972 Elvis Summer Festival** at the Las Vegas Hilton.

Wait! There are some records here that aren't by Elvis! Who is **Vince Everett**? It's the rockin' singer that Elvis played in his movie *Jailhouse Rock* (1957). These 45 rpm sleeves are some of the records that "Vince" put out. They are actually **props** from the movie. Speaking of *Jailhouse Rock*, can you find the three times that **this title** appears in the scene? How about the nine times that it appears in this whole book?

The *Janis & Elvis* album was released in 1958 in South Africa and was on the market for just a few days until Colonel Parker found out about it and complained about Elvis sharing the billing. The King didn't actually sing any duets with **Janis Darlene Martin** on this album, which featured six songs from each. She was an 18-year-old from Sutherlin, Virginia who was also a rock & roll singer on the RCA label whose career was also off to a fast start in the mid-1950s. Unlike Elvis, she faded just as quickly as she took off.

The **sailor cap** is an original, purchased from **Lansky Brothers** at 126 Beale Street in Memphis. This was where Elvis bought his clothes and these types of caps which he liked to wear while boating. The store is no longer in existence. There are 23 **guitars** in this picture *(only one of them is real)*, two **guitar picks** and two **drumsticks**. Can you see them all?

The **scarves** and the **embroidered "Elvis the King" jacket** draped over the chair is from a fan club in England. There are also 48 cloth patches, including three **"TCB"** patches. The initials stand for **Taking Care of Business** and the lightning bolt means **Taking Care of Business in a *flash***. That was Elvis' motto.

All of the patches are from England except the **TCB patches** and the **"Elvis in Concert" patch**, which is from the red leather and suede jackets worn by his tour bodyguards. Elvis designed one of these TCB patches himself for his karate uniform when he was studying karate with Master Kang Rhee in the early 1970s. He earned his black belt in Tae Kwon Do from Master Kang Rhee and in Kenpo karate from Ed Parker, but who is this pointing to this patch?

OUR FANTASY ELVIS BEDROOM

In the **Memphis** of our mind there is a little wood frame home on US Highway 51 South. (They call it **Elvis Presley Boulevard** now.) In that house there is a bedroom where we are surrounded by the memorabilia that helps us visualize our dreams.

One **tapestry** is a tribute to the **stamp** that was issued by the US Postal Service on the 58th anniversary of his birth in another wood frame home, across a state line but not far from Memphis. The **poster** next to the tapestry was issued two decades before, when he was still with us.

The **hound dogs** are, for the most part, souvenirs of his appearances at the **Las Vegas Hilton** during the 1970s. Of course no bedroom is complete without teddy bears—especially an *Elvis* bedroom. After his mega-hit song *Teddy Bear* was released in 1957, people sent him thousands of teddy bears for his collection. Can you find the four pictured in this scene?

The **bedspread** and **matching pillow** are from the memorabilia created for the **First Annual Elvis Fan Reunion** in 1978 at the Las Vegas Hilton. It was a ten-day affair that was supposed to be repeated every year, but it happened only once!

The *Love Me Tender* conditioning shampoo appeared only briefly in the mid-1980s. This product is hard to find now, but not nearly as hard to find as the *Love Me Tender* candy bars (not pictured, sorry) that came out in 1956.

There are **buttons** here commemorating the fifth, sixth, ninth and tenth anniversaries of his death. Do you see them? Can you find 28 other **buttons** here?

There are nine **guitars** here. Do you see them all? There's only *one* **guitar** that Elvis would be able to pick up and pluck if he came to sit on the edge of the bed and hum *The Wonder of You*. It's not much of a guitar, but it's a prized reminder of the kinds of souvenirs that were released to commemorate the King of Rock & Roll. (The snapshot is of Robin and **Elvis' Uncle Vester** taken on her first trip to Memphis.)

PICTURES FROM ELVIS' PICTURE SHOWS

Elvis made four movies in 1956-1958 before he went into the Army, and in 1960 he went back to **Hollywood**. Over the next ten years, he starred in another 27 motion pictures. After 1970, the only Elvis films were documentaries. This scene is a tribute to those Hollywood years.

One of his greatest and best-remembered movies was *Jailhouse Rock* (1957), in which he co-starred with Judy Tyler. There is an **original poster** for this film in the scene along with ten **other pictures**. Can you see them all?

His first-ever co-star was **Debra Paget**, and he starred opposite **Mary Tyler Moore** in *Change of Habit* (1970), his last dramatic film. They're both pictured here. Can you find them?

Twenty years after Elvis was in Hollywood, the band Mojo Nixon did a song called **Elvis Is Everywhere**, in which they sang about how Elvis needed boats! He also liked **cars**, and they figured in his movies such as *Viva Las Vegas* (1964), *Spinout* (1966) and *Speedway* (1968). Can you find 11 **cars** pictured in this scene? Can you find six **buttons** with pictures from his movies and one button with a picture of **Colonel Tom Parker**? How about two **guitar picks**, six **six-shooters** and twelve **guitars**?

Did you know that *Burning Love* was a brand name for those **hot stage lights** that actors are always complaining about? Actually, it's not. We're just kidding.

The **blue suede jacket** was owned by Elvis in the early 1970s. Robin has a picture of him wearing it over his jumpsuit as he's walking into the Houston Astrodome on February 27, 1970. She picked this up at a Sisters of the Holy Family auction. She got into a bidding war with another fan, but she saw that the handwritten "E. Presley" inside the left breast pocket was authentic and she said to herself "I'm coming home with this if it's the last thing I do!"

She did, but it wasn't.

ALOHA FROM BLUE HAWAII

Elvis loved **Hawaii**. He loved the people. He loved the weather. He loved the boats. He loved the food and he loved the beaches.

He first went to the Islands to do a benefit for the USS *Arizona* memorial in 1961, which was the same year he filmed *Blue Hawaii*. He went back in 1966 to film *Paradise Hawaiian Style*. When it came time for the biggest rock concert in history, he picked Hawaii to host it. His January 14, 1973 *Aloha From Hawaii* show was simulcast via satellite to *half a billion* fans in 40 countries! (Can you find a picture of the **satellite** here?)

This scene recreates the fun of Elvis' Hawaiian paradise. You'll want to fix yourself a cool drink like those pictured here (don't forget to use *two* paper umbrellas), and curl up on your favorite beach mat to enjoy this corner of Robin's collection. You'll also want to find a **Hawaiian Christmas card** sent out by Elvis and Colonel Parker, a picture of **Elvis and Priscilla** on their Hawaiian honeymoon in 1967 and a picture of Elvis—wearing a **floppy hat** and sunglasses—from his last-ever Hawaiian vacation just ten years later. Also find the pewter *Blue Hawaii* memorial statuette issued shortly after he passed away. The **TV magazine** is from Australia—from the *other* side of the blue Pacific!

You might like to also try to find: Fifteen **stringed musical instruments** (wasn't it *great* when he played the ukelele?) and remember when **Elvis played drums** in *Blue Hawaii*. Can you find that pictured here? Also try to find him in the *same* swimming trunks five times.

On the way to finding these treasures, you might trip over some things that fans have dropped here on the beach, like an **Elvis Memorial Fan Club Hawaii button** or a **ticket** to the January 14, 1973 concert or a set of **hotel keys**. Or maybe they're the keys to *his* hotel room, or the keys to his *heart*.

And then there's the **bottle** washed up on the beach. Maybe Elvis threw it into the water for *us* to find.

ELVIS ON THE LAS VEGAS STAGE

Elvis is remembered as a consummate stage performer—especially for those incredible shows in **Las Vegas** that he did twice a year during the 1970s. From the time he went into the Army in 1958 until his *Comeback Special* on TV ten years later, he'd been on stage only a few times. Then, in July 1969, Colonel Parker booked him into the new **Las Vegas International Hotel** for a month-long stand. It was like nothing Vegas had ever seen. Many people had written off Elvis as a "has been," but suddenly, he was the hottest show on Earth!

This scene celebrates Elvis during the peak of his performance career—on stage in Las Vegas, at Lake Tahoe and elsewhere. The two taller **Elvis statues** on the left and right were purchased by Robin shortly after Elvis died, from a lady who made them by hand. The small Elvis statue—the one where he's holding a microphone cord and wearing a red scarf—is actually a transistor radio. Imagine... a **singing Elvis statue** that also reads you the news!

The **squirt gun** is a memento from when Robin and some of her friends had the on-stage "shoot out" with Elvis that's mentioned in the books *Inside Elvis* and *Jailhouse Rock*. Everybody started shooting at Elvis when he was on stage. Then Robin gave a squirt gun to Elvis and *he* started shooting back!

Elvis said it was like the gunfight at the OK Corral. It's a wonder that nobody got electrocuted.

Can you find an **autographed napkin**, a **styrofoam straw hat** from the **1970 Elvis Summer Festival** at the Las Vegas Hilton, six **Sahara Tahoe tickets** and a **handbill** announcing one of only a couple of his **Special 3 a.m. Shows** that he gave?

Everybody knew that Elvis was *the* King. Can you find four **kings**? There are a lot of **gaming chips** here, but only a single **one dollar chip** from the **International Hotel**. In the snapshot where Elvis is wearing a blue jumpsuit he is with **Rhonda Aiken** and her friends. Rhonda's license plate number is "ELVIS 6." Robin's is "ELVIS 7." They met when they parked their cars next to one another at a grocery store. The other snapshot shows Elvis with **Red West** *(left)* and **Sonny West** *(right)*. They were cousins from Memphis who worked for Elvis for many years.

One of the more valuable mementos here is the **gold-plated, brass Elvis Presley show-member ID card** from the early 1970s. This is one of a handful of blanks still in existence that was never stamped with the person's name and their position within the entourage. There were only about 85 people in the entourage.

The **champagne glass** is a memento of May 9, 1976 at the **Sahara Tahoe**, when Robin was partying with the maitre d' and several friends on closing night and Elvis sent down champagne. Robin saw Elvis 63 times in Las Vegas and seven times at Tahoe, and she's got the scarves and photos to prove it! The picture here of him kissing a lady in the audience—well, *that's* Robin!

AN ELVIS JEWELRY BOX

Some of the best examples of **Elvis** memorabilia are those that we can hold close to our hearts—just as we hold the man close to our hearts. There's even one item here that you might have been given for running **just over three miles in Memphis**. Do you see it?

Included here is an original **"Tender Loving Care (TLC)"** necklace with a chain with no clasp. Elvis had the necklace designed this way because to him this implied the never-ending bond of friendship.

His motto was **"Taking Care of Business,"** and the initials **"TCB"** appear wherever he is remembered. Can you find three items with "TCB" here? (Hint: The **jewel-encrusted item** is a replica of the one worn by Elvis himself.) Speaking of words, can you find the names of six of his songs mentioned a total of eight times?

Can you find a big button from the fan club of an **American city** and the **fan club badge** in the shape of a sheriff's badge from a fan club in England? The biggest item here is a solid sterling silver **Canadian medallion** paying tribute to the King.

How about two **buttons** from 1956 that work his name into the slogan from the campaign of the man who was elected president that year? We'll give you a hint: His vice president had the same *last* name as the band that put out the **"Elvis Needs Boats"** buttons. Can you find one of those?

There are a lot of tributes to Elvis and his life in this scene. Do you see his **birth date** mentioned nine times? Do you see the **pillow** made by Gail Alien in the Haight Ashbury? We'll give you a clue: It's right next to a button with something that you might have found on Elvis' real pillow. It's not actually from his pillow but from March 25, 1958—the day Elvis went into the Army.

ELVIS ON OUR REFRIGERATOR

Elvis is everywhere. He's in our hearts and he's on the lips of everyone. He's in our minds and he's on our refrigerators. He's in many of these snapshots and so are some of his friends.

Do you see him in his airplane with **Linda Thompson**? In his car with **Joe Esposito**? Doing karate with **Red West**? Or him on **water skis** during the shooting of *Clambake* in 1967?

Who are these people? Linda Thompson held the titles of Miss Memphis State and Miss Liberty Bowl before becoming runner-up in the Miss USA Pageant. She lived with Elvis from 1972, when he broke up with Priscilla, until 1976.

Joe Esposito, whom Elvis called "Diamond Joe," met the King when they were in the Army together in Germany and became his road manager in 1960. Joe became one of the most trusted members of Elvis' entourage, and was with him until he died in 1977.

Red West was one of Elvis' closest friends from their early days in Memphis and he was part of the King's entourage from 1955—when he volunteered to drive Elvis' band to their live shows—until 1976.

Do you see Elvis with Robin when she was wearing the coat that's on the cover of this book?

Can you find **Elvis and Priscilla with Lisa Marie** when Lisa was less than a year old? When you find that one, the lady in the corner with the "Roy Orbison glasses" is Elvis' grandma, "Dodger." Dodger's real name was **Minnie Mae Hood Presley**. She was Vernon Presley's mama and she outlived both he and Elvis. She got the nickname because when Elvis was five years old, he got cranky and threw a baseball at her. She dodged the ball and was ever after known as "Dodger."

Can you find a magnet from the **24-hour Church of Elvis** in Portland, Oregon?

If Elvis was living in **Kalamazoo** in 1988, why was this letter marked **"Return to Sender"**?

THE DESKTOP ELVIS

This is a really messy desk, but don't you wish *your* desk had some of this stuff on it?

There are at least 29 of the 29-cent stamps that the US Postal Service issued on January 8, 1993, and several pictures of it. Remember back in 1992 when we all voted for the picture we wanted them to put on the stamp? More people voted for the *King's stamp* than voted for the *president* in 1992! Can you find a picture here of the *other* design, the one that we rejected? Can you find the Elvis stamps from **Palau**? From **St. Vincent**? The **"Return to Sender"** envelope was stamped at the **Las Vegas Hilton** on Elvis' 58th birthday.

There are five animals here, four of which are important to the **Elvis legend**: The **hound dog** from the 1956 song; the **teddy bear** from the 1957 song; **Nipper**, the RCA mascot; and **"Tiger,"** which was Elvis' karate name. **"Elmoose Presley"** is a strange artifact that Robin found in 1988. It's good for a laugh, and a valuable collector's item.

Whew! Normally we don't much care for paperwork, but there's a lot of wonderful Elvis paperwork here... like one of the *original* **title search documents** for a house in Southern California that is signed by *both* Elvis and Priscilla. There's also a copy of the **pink slip** (registration) for one of his motorcycles. He registered this bike in **Palm Springs** at the white stucco house that he bought in 1965 and willed to Lisa Marie. It was sold to Frankie Valli of the Four Seasons in 1979 for more than three times what Elvis paid. There's also a copy of the **deed** to the house that Elvis bought in March 1957 at 3764 US Highway 51 South in Memphis. Although Elvis lived in a lot of houses, this would be his home for the next twenty years and his final resting place. Can you see twelve places where the gates to this house appear in the scene?

Elvis was the **King**, but he was also the **deputy**—of the Shelby County, Tennessee, Sheriff's Department! Can you find two artifacts here from that association? We'll give you a hint: The badge is *not* one of them. Now it's easy.

Speaking of Tennessee, can you find the Madison, Tennessee address for the man who appears here in the **Santa Claus** suit? Robin never got a Christmas card from *this* man, but she *did* get a card from Elvis in 1973 thanking her for sending a **get well card** when he was ill with fatigue and intestinal problems. Can you find it?

THE ELVIS GAME ROOM

Don't you wish you could play here all day and all night? It would be almost like being able to live **Elvis**' life right along with him... from Tupelo to the time he was the King of Rock & Roll... and until tomorrow, and forever.

Speaking of Tupelo, can you find the **year** that his name was first spoken in that Mississippi town? **Tupelo** is mentioned here six times. Can you find them all?

Elvis was the King of Rock & Roll. Can you see him pictured here with a **crown**, and four times as the **King of Hearts**? Can you find him twice more as the King of Hearts in another part of this book? If Elvis was the *King*, who was the *Boss*? Can you find **him** pictured here?

There's a lot of "funny money" in the Game Room, and there's also a replica of a **check** from his personal account. The original check was used to buy one of many cars that he purchased for friends, such as Lamar Fike, the member of his entourage who Elvis referred to as "Buddha."

Speaking of cars, can you find the **pink Cadillac**, two mentions of **other Cadillacs**, and a reference to his **two "car race" movies**?

Elvis liked to pass out **scarves** to his fans at concerts. Can you find two references to scarves? (This is not including the pictures of Elvis wearing scarves.)

While you were looking for those, did you happen to trip over four **guitar picks**, a **teddy bear**, a **golden image** of the King holding a guitar and a *Love Me Tender* marble?

Jerry Leiber and Mike Stoller were two of the hottest rock & roll songwriters of the 1950s, and maybe of all time. Among their songs that Elvis recorded were *Baby I Don't Care*, *Bossa Nova Baby*, *Hound Dog*, *Jailhouse Rock*, *King Creole*, *Treat Me Nice* and *Trouble*. They also wrote **another** famous song that Elvis did *not* record. Its title was the name of an American city mentioned in this display from the Elvis Game Room. Where is it?

The next time you hear Elvis singing *Let's Play House*, imagine that the house has got a Game Room like this one in it!

THE ELVIS LIBRARY

Actually this is just a small part of Robin's **Elvis library**, but it's a good representation. How many of these do you have?

As we were sitting in this corner of Robin's library talking about the King, we realized how remarkable it was that Elvis was known to so many by his first name. Other superstars like Cher, Madonna and Liberace worked hard at getting themselves known by one name, but with Elvis, it just came about *naturally*. In this scene alone, his first name outnumbers mention of his surname by 112 to 25!

After you've had a chance to sit down in your blue suede easy chair and browse through all these books, and wish *you* had a library like this one, take a look and see if you can find nine **guitars**, four **pink Cadillacs**, three **guitar picks**, two **infamous politicians**, an **Elvis pencil**, a **blue suede shoe**, two **shoelaces**, a **teddy bear**, a **Scandinavian Elvis book** and a **book** that appears *twice*.

There are also three **books** here that **Elvis movies** are based on (*Jailhouse Rock* is *not* one) and one book that's *related* to Elvis by the fact that it was one of his **favorites**... can you find these? Can you find the book by his **nurse**?

His **high school** is pictured once and mentioned once, and there's an Elvis **license plate**.

Can you also find a *real* bottle of **Teddy Bear Parfum** and a phony (but funny) **Elvis thumb print**?

In among the books are three **busts**: The darkest one was made of bronze in Canada in the early 1970s. The white one was one of the keepsakes available for purchase at the one and only **First Annual Elvis Fan Reunion** that was held at the Las Vegas Hilton in 1978.

The gold bust is one of the rarest mementos in Robin's collection. It is solid brass and one of only a handful that were produced in 1961 at the time that his seventh film *Wild in the Country* was released.

The **caricature** on the left is a memento from May 25, 1974, when Robin and her friend Jill saw Elvis at the **Sahara Tahoe**. Can you find them in the front row?

26

THE ELVIS KITCHEN

Welcome to Robin's **kitchen**. This is the *ultimate* **Elvis** fantasy kitchen. It's the kind of kitchen that you find in the homes of folks who still set a place for Elvis at their tables each night.

For this photo, the food was prepared by Brenda Arlene Butler who developed the cookbook *Are You Hungry Tonight?* As she wrote in her book, "Elvis was Southern-born and Southern-bred. His culinary tastes never varied far from Southern-style home cooking. If Elvis were to come into your own dining room tonight he'd say, 'Yes, ma'am,' and 'Thank you, ma'am,' and probably ask for the same kind of good home cooking that his mother, Gladys, put on the table in Tupelo, Mississippi in the late 1930s. Gladys cooked all the traditional Southern favorites. Grits and black-eyed peas were served, ham and bacon were an occasional treat, and there was always fried chicken, cornbread, chili, dogs and kraut, mashed potatoes and plenty of homemade country gravy."

These were among the King's favorite foods. He also liked ripe, thickly sliced **beefsteak tomatoes**. His favorite food, though, was **Fried Peanut Butter & Banana Sandwiches** (he called them Peanut Butter & *'Nanner* Sandwiches), and there's one cooking here on Robin's stove.

Also in this yummy picture, find 33 **guitars**, four **drumsticks**, two pictures of **Priscilla**, a **"TCB" shot glass**, a picture of Elvis with **Lisa Marie**, and five pictures of Elvis getting ready to **eat**.

The picture in the upper lefthand corner with Elvis wearing the "Roy Orbison glasses" dates from the late 1960s and it's actually a **place mat**. The **black tray** on the stove was a memento that was produced in South Africa!

In the picture where Elvis is holding a **gun**, the guys that are second from the outside on both sides of the table are **Scotty Moore** *(left)* and **Bill Black** *(right)*, two of Elvis' most loyal sidemen. Who is the state trooper? Can you find a memento from **The Hound Dog Cafe** which used to be located at 3717 Elvis Presley Boulevard?

The four **decanters** are part of a series produced by McCormick Distillers from the late 1970s to the early 1980s. There are a total of eight bottles here of **Always Elvis** and **A Portrait of Elvis** wine. Elvis didn't actually drink wine, but in 1978, somebody got the idea to market an Elvis tribute wine. It was *blanc d'oro* (white gold) and made in Italy for Frontenac Vineyards of Dearborn, Michigan by CVBC&C of Fossalta. It's a lot harder to find on the market now than it is in this picture.

THE ULTIMATE ELVIS SHRINE

We all have an **Elvis** shrine, whether it's in a place in our home or our record cabinet devoted to mementos of personal experience with Elvis and his music, or a place in our heart devoted to our special feelings for the King. Come now and spend a quiet moment with *this* shrine amid the smell of **burning candles** and the memories of **burning love**.

The **rose** that occupies the prominent central place in this scene was one of a dozen that were preserved by the florist who made the casket cover for Elvis' funeral, and given to Robin personally by the florist in 1978. The red rose in the foreground is from the mausoleum at Forest Hill Cemetery in Memphis where Elvis' body was interred from August 16 to October 2, 1977.

The **trophy** on the right was won by Robin at the Fan Club Presidents' Luncheon in Memphis during Tribute Week in August 1992. The card below the trophy was given to Robin by the Presley family in appreciation for the sympathy card and flowers that she sent when Elvis passed away in 1977.

For Elvis, **2001** was a number with special significance. If you add the numerals of the day (16), month (8) and year (1977) that Elvis died, it totals 2001. If you add the day that he was born (8), to the year that he was born (1935), the day he died (16), and the age that he was when he died (42), it also totals 2001. Elvis used the composition *Also Sprach Zarathustra*, the theme from the 1969 film *2001: A Space Odyssey*, as the opening music for his shows.

The **lock of Elvis' hair** in the lucite frame was given to Robin by Fran Hagen, her friend from Pasadena, Texas, who got it from Elvis' barber. The Bible is open to *one* of Elvis' favorite passages from the Book of Revelation, chapter 21, verses 2-27. Also in this tribute you can search for three **teddy bears**, 11 **guitars** (including a **guitar** *within* a guitar), three references to the **city where he was born** (or the **Memorial Chapel** located in that city), five references to the **year that he passed away**, and three references to the **Annual Candlelight Service**.

The Annual Candlelight Service originated with the Elvis Country Fan Club of Austin, Texas and is held every year in Memphis in August. There are usually as many as 10,000 people in attendance, and in 1987, on the tenth anniversary of his death, there were over 50,000. It is a very solemn affair beginning at 10 o'clock in the evening and lasting until 5 o'clock the next morning. Elvis Presley Boulevard is closed off, torches are lit from the Elvis eternal flame and people file past, each lighting his or her own candle from the torches. All the while, Elvis songs are being played over several speakers on the grounds. The procession courses through the Meditation Garden to Elvis' grave where everyone pays their respects.

LADIES AND GENTLEMEN...
    ELVIS HAS LEFT THE BUILDING."